NEW Grammar Time 1

Contents

The alphabet, numbers — 4

1 *a /an*, plurals — 6

2 *be*, subject pronouns — 12

Use your English (Units 1-2) — 18

3 *this, that, these, those* — 20

4 Prepositions of place — 26

5 *There is, There are* — 30

Use your English (Units 3-5) — 34

6 Possessive adjectives — 36

7 Possessive 's — 40

8 *have got* — 44

9 *can* — 50

Use your English (Units 6-9) — 54

10 Imperatives — 56

11 Present simple — 60

12 *have / has* — 66

Use your English (Units 10-12) — 70

13 Prepositions of time, *when* — 72

14 Question words — 76

15 Present continuous — 80

Use your English (Units 13-15) — 86

Grammar Reference — 88

Word List — 94

3

🎧 The alphabet

'C' is for Corky!

🎧 Numbers

1 Write the first letter and find the name of the animal.

1 ...G...orilla
3 ....nsect
3 ....abbit
4 ....lligator
5 ....ish
6 ....ox
7 ....lephant

The animal is a : G _ _ _ _ _ _

2 Write, draw and find the number.

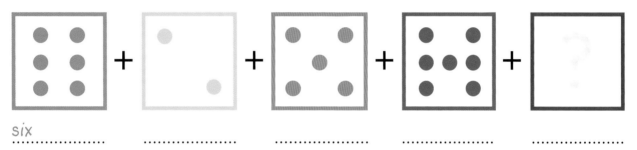

six ....

3 Read the code and find the secret phrase.

A=1   B=2   C=3   D=4   E=5   F=6   H=7   I=8   K=9
N=10   O=11   R=12   T=13   U=14   V=15   W=16   Y=17   Z=18

seven   one   fifteen   five
....
six   fourteen   ten
....
sixteen   eight   thirteen   seven
....
eighteen   eleven   five
....
two   twelve   eight   one   ten
....
four   one   fifteen   five
....
one   ten   four
....
three   eleven   twelve   nine   seventeen
....

a / an, plurals

a / an, *-s* plurals

1 | a book | seven books

2 | an orange | four oranges

3 | an ant | twenty ants

4 | a toy | three toys

- Consonants: b c d f g h j k l m n p q r s t v w x y z
- Vowels: a e i o u

a + consonants	*an* + vowels	Singular	Plural (+ -s)
a book	**an** apple	**a** book	two book**s**
a fish	**an** egg	**a** toy	four toy**s**
a toy	**an** igloo	**an** orange	five orange**s**
a hat	**an** orange	**an** ant	twenty ant**s**
a window	**an** umbrella		

1 Draw lines and match.

iguana · ostrich · frog · apple · elephant · cat · window · zebra · kite · umbrella

2 Look and write *a* or *an*.

1 *a* .... friend
2 *an* .... egg
3 .... octopus
4 .... pen
5 .... rubber
6 .... alligator
7 .... elephant
8 .... teacher
9 .... bag
10 .... cat

3 Write.

1 a bag   three *bags* ....
2 a cake   four ....
3 a boy   six ....
4 a frog   ten ....
5 an apple   twenty ....
6 a girl   seven ....
7 a bee   twenty ....
8 a window   nine ....
9 a ball   five ....
10 an eye   two ....

a / an, -es plurals

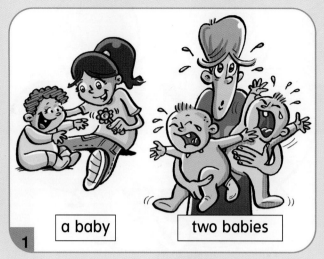

1 | a baby | two babies

2 | a box | five boxes

3 | a glass | two glasses

4 | a tomato | three tomatoes

Singular	Plural (+ -es)
a bus	two buses
a glass	three glasses
a brush	four brushes
a watch	five watches
a box	six boxes
a tomato	seven tomatoes

Singular	Plural (-y → -ies)
a baby	two babies
a cherry	four cherries

Singular	Plural (-y → -ys)
a boy	ten boys
a toy	seven toys

▶ Look at the spelling rules on page 88.

4 **Look, count and write.**

tree

1 *two trees* ....

tomato

2 ....

glass

3 ....

kite

4 ....

witch

5 ....

monkey

6 ....

brush

7 ....

potato

8 ....

watch

9 ....

5 **Write the plural.**

a fox   ~~an iguana~~   a cherry   a boy   a box   an alligator

a dress   a bus   a bee   a strawberry   a baby

-s	-es	-ies
1 *iguanas*	5	9 ....
2	6	10 ....
3	7	11 ....
4	8	

1 a mouse

2 eleven mice

3 a child

4 nine children

Singular	Plural
child	children
man	men
woman	women
tooth	teeth
foot	feet
mouse	mice

Singular	Plural
sheep	sheep
fish	fish

Irregular nouns change in different ways in the plural.

Some irregular nouns don't change in the plural.

6 **Look and write the plural.**

1 mouse ....*mice*........   2 man ....   3 foot ....

4 child ....   5 sheep ....   6 tooth ....

7 **Write.**

1 a man   (6) ...*six men*........   6 a foot   (10) ....
2 a desk   (3) ...*three desks*...   7 a mouse   (3) ....
3 a fish   (12) ....   8 a cherry   (8) ....
4 a woman   (2) ....   9 a tooth   (13) ....
5 a baby   (4).....................   10 a glass   (6) ....

8 **Look, count and say.**

three children
one cherry

2 *be*, subject pronouns

I am, you are (negative, question)

Positive		Negative	
I am I'm	a ballerina. pretty.	I am not I'm not	a bird. OK.
You are You're		You are not You aren't	

Questions		Short answers
Am I	pretty? OK?	Yes, you are. No, you are not. / No, you aren't.
Are you		Yes, I am. No, I am not. / No, I'm not.

- When we speak, we use short forms: I'm, you're, I'm not, you aren't.
- We use short forms to answer *no*: No, I'm not.   No, you aren't.
- But we use long forms to answer *yes*: Yes, I am. ✔ Yes, I'm. ✗
                                          Yes, you are. ✔ Yes, you're. ✗

1 Write *am* or *are*.

1 I ...am... Dave.
2 You .... not happy.

3 .... you happy?
4 .... I seven?

2 Write the short form.

1 You are happy.   *You're happy.*
2 I am not ten.   ....
3 You are not sad.   ....
4 I am silly!   ....

3 Circle the correct words.

1 I'm / (Am I) a teacher?
2 You're / Are you ten?
3 I'm / Am I eight.

4 I'm / Am I good?
5 You're / Are you OK.
6 I'm / Are you a bird?

4 Look, read and write.

1 ...Am... I clever?
Yes, you ....

2 .... you sad?
Yes, I ....

3 .... I a boy?
No, you............ !

4 .... I good?
Yes, you ....!

5 .... you Corky?
No, I............ not.

6 .... I your friend?
Yes, you ....

5 Ask and answer.

Are you ten?   Yes, I am.

1 ten?
2 happy?
3 a pupil?
4 a bird?
5 a teacher?
6 clever?

Now swap roles.

he / she / it is (negative, question)

Panel 1: Look! It's a new CD. — Oh! Rex Rock?

Panel 2: Is he a good singer? — Yes, he is. He's very good. Listen!

Panel 3: Oh, no! He isn't good! He's terrible!

Panel 4: She's mad!

Positive		
He She It	is 's	a good singer. a CD.

Negative		
He She It	is not isn't	a good singer. a CD.

Questions		
Is	he she it	a good singer? a CD?

Short answers		
Yes,	he she	is.
No,	it	isn't.

= he

= she

= it

6 Write *He's*, *She's* or *It's*.

1 (Zoe) *She's* happy.
2 (Brian) .... clever.
3 (the CD) .... new.

4 (the girl) .... tall.
5 (the mouse) .... grey.
6 (the man) .... a teacher.

7 Read and write.

1 Brian is tall. No, Brian *isn't* tall. He *'s* short.
2 The cat is black. No, the cat .... black. It .... grey.
3 Corky is a girl. No, Corky .... a girl. He .... a boy!
4 Zoe is ten. No, Zoe .... ten. She .... nine.
5 The box is big. No, the box .... big. It .... small.
6 Dave is silly. No, Dave .... silly. He .... funny!

8 Read and write.

1
.... a bird? *Is it*
No, ...
.... a plane.

.... a cowboy?
Yes, ...

3
.... good?
No, ...
.... bad!

4
.... funny?
Yes, ...

9 Ask and answer.

Is your friend tall?

No, he isn't. He's short.

1 tall?   2 funny?   3 a teacher?   4 eight?

Now swap roles.

we / you / they are (question, negative)

Dave, Zoe! Are you here?

Yes, we are!

1

Surprise!

2

Wow!

3

You're great!

They're very good friends.

4

Positive		
We You They	are 're	friends. here.

Negative		
We You They	are not aren't	friends. here.

Questions		
Are	we you they	friends? here?

Short answers		
Yes,	we you they	are.
No,		aren't.

Singular		Plural
I	➡	we
you	➡	you
he, she, it	➡	they

10 Write, *We're*, *You're* or *They're*.

1 Dave and I / friends.   *We're* .... friends.
2 Zoe and Brian / not sad.   *They aren't* .... sad.
3 The CDs / good.   .... good.
4 My friend and I / pupils.   .... pupils.
5 You and Brian / hungry.   .... hungry.
6 The lions / big.   .... big.

11 Write questions and answers.

1 they / pupils?   *Are they pupils?* ....   Yes, they are.
2 you / teachers?   Are you teachers?   No, *we aren't.* ....
3 we / bad?   ....   No, you aren't.
4 you / hungry?   Are you hungry?   Yes, ...
5 we / short?   ....   No, you aren't.
6 they / good?   Are they good?   No, ...

12 Look, read and write.

.... *They're happy!*

....

....

1 they / happy!   2 we / hungry   3 it / small

....

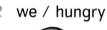
....

....

4 you / not / bad.   5 she / not / funny!   6 it / black and white.
you / good!   it / a panda?

13 Play a game. What is it? Take turns.

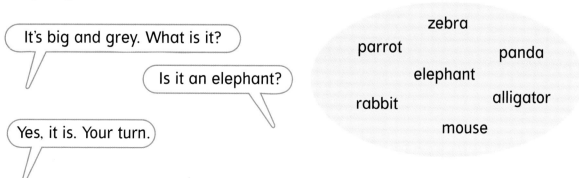

It's big and grey. What is it?

Is it an elephant?

Yes, it is. Your turn.

zebra
parrot   panda
elephant
rabbit   alligator
mouse

Use your English (Units 1–2)

1 **Look, ask and answer. Then write.**

1 2 3 4 5 6

One. What is it?   It's an iguana.

1 It's .....*an iguana.*.....   4 It's ....

2 It's ....   5 It's ....

3 It's ....   6 It's ....

2 **Count and say. Then write.**

1 .....*ten cherries*.....   4 ....

2 ....   5 ....

3 ....   6 ....

3 **Listen and tick ✔.**

1 A Zoe is happy. ☐
   B Zoe isn't happy. ☐

2 A Brian is a good singer. ☐
   B Brian is a bad singer. ☐

3 A It's an iguana. ☐
   B It's an alligator. ☐

4 A The classroom is big. ☐
   B The classroom is small. ☐

5 A The cherries are good. ☐
   B The cherries are bad. ☐

6 A They are good friends. ☐
   B They aren't good friends. ☐

4 **Look and read. Put a tick ✔ or a cross ✗ in the box.**

1 They aren't frogs. ✔

2 She is fifteen. ✗

3 They are short. ☐

4 He isn't a pupil. ☐

5 They aren't old. ☐

6 It is red. ☐

5 **Ask and answer.**

1 ...Is............ Zoe six?   No, she isn't. She's nine.
2 ...Are........... alligators green?   Yes, they are.
3 .... teeth purple?   ....
4 .... Dave short?   ....
5 .... strawberries brown?   ....
6 .... Corky a bird?   ....
7 .... I a teacher?   ....
8 .... you nine?   ....

Now you can ...

✔ Introduce yourself.
Hello, I'm Sam.
✔ Talk about people, animals or things.
Anna is my friend.
Is the dog happy?
The cherries aren't good.

3 this, that, these, those

this / that

1

> Now, Corky, this is a watch. OK?

> OK.

2

> That is a clock.

> Aha …

3

> This is a photo.

4

> … and that is a picture!

> Oh! It's a good picture!

Singular		
This ➡	is	a watch.
That ➡		a clock.

- We use *this* + a singular verb to talk about something near.
- We use *that* + a singular verb to talk about something far.

20

1 Circle the correct word.

1 **(This)** / That is a horse.

2 This / **(That)** is a zebra.

3 This / That is a boy.

4 This / That is an iguana.

5 This / That is a bag.

6 This / That is a fish.

7 This / That is a baby.

8 This / That is an apple.

2 Look and write questions and answers.

1 *Is this* .... a T-shirt
Yes, it is. ....

2 *Is that* .... a watch?
No, it isn't. ....

3 .... a school bag?
....

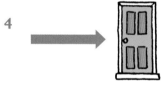

4 .... a door?
....

5 .... a chair?
....

6 .... a CD?
....

3 Test your partner. Take turns.

1 Is this a pencil?

Is that a door?

Yes, it is.

No, it isn't.

These are pandas here.

Those are bears over there.

These are chimps and those are gorillas.

Yes, all right Corky!

These are sandwiches and those are burgers over there.

Oh, be quiet, Corky!

this / these

Singular	This ➡	is	a panda.
Plural	These ➡	are	pandas.

that / these

Singular	That ➡	is	a bear.
Plural	Those ➡	are	bears.

4 Write *these* or *those*.

1 ....*These*.... are happy children.

2 ....*Those*.... are sad children.

3 .... are red kites.

4 .... are green kites.

5 .... are small T-shirts.

6 .... are big T-shirts.

7 .... are green dinosaurs.

8 .... are brown dinosaurs.

5 Write *is* or *are*.

1 This ....*is*.... a big car.
2 Those ....*are*.... good pictures.
3 That .... a small window.

4 These .... red pens.
5 Those .... green apples.
6 This .... a clever dog.

6 Look, ask and answer. Take turns.

1 green birds?
2 a frog?
3 white bears?
4 a chimp?
5 a big fish?
6 iguanas?

Are these green birds?

Yes, they are.

Is this a frog?

No, it isn't. It's an iguana.

3 What is / What are

1. What's this? — It's a schoolbag!

2. What's that? — It's a pencil.

3. What are these? — They're shoes!

4. What are those? — They're books.

5. What's that?

6. Grrgh! Mmmph!

Singular	What's this? It's a schoolbag.
Plural	What are these? They're shoes.

Singular	What's that? It's a pencil.
Plural	What are those? They're books.

- We answer the question *What's this / that?* with *It's … .*
- We answer the question *What are these / those?* with *They're … .*

7 Look, choose and write.

~~this~~   these   that   those   It's   They're

1
What's *this* ....?

It's .... a clock.

2
What's ....?

.... a picture.

3
What are ....?

.... bees.

4
What are ....?

.... school bags.

5
What's ....?

.... a plane.

6
What are ....?

.... cherries.

8 Ask and answer. Take turns.

What's this?

It's a hat.

❶

What are those?

They're fish.

❷

❸

❹

❺

❻

❼

❽

Prepositions of place			
	in		next to
	on		in front of
	under		near
	behind		

Where	is 's	he? she? it?
He She It	's	under the table. in the box. in front of the sofa.

1 Circle the correct word(s).

1 Corky is in / (under) the bed.

2 Zoe is on / behind Dave.

3 Brian is behind / next to Zoe.

4 Corky is on / in the box.

5 Zoe is on / under the table.

6 Corky is in front of / next to Dave.

2 Look, read and write.

1 Where's Zoe?
She's ...*in*...... the bus.

2 Where's the CD?
It's .... the table.

3 Where's the ball?
It's .... the car.

4 Where's the car?
It's .... the house.

5 Where's the rubber?
It's .... the desk.

6 Where's Brian?
He's .... the door.

7 Where's the school?
It's .... the park.

27

Where is, Where are

Singular

Where is …? Where's … ?	It's / He's / She's … .

Where's the vase? It's on the table.

Plural

Where are … ?	They're …

Where are the flowers? They're in the vase.

3 Look, choose and write.

> in on (x2) under behind (x2) in front of next to

1 Where's Brian?   He's ....behind.... the table.
2 Where's the birthday cake?   It's ....on....... the table.
3 Where are the flowers?   They're .... the vase.
4 Where are the toy cars?   They're .... the table.
5 Where's Corky?   He's .... the two girls.
6 Where's Zoe?   She's .... the sofa.
7 Where's Dave?   He's .... Zoe.
8 Where are the presents?   They're .... the sofa.

4 Write *Where's*, *Where are*, *It's* or *They're*.

1 ..Where's.............. the TV?   ..It's........ on the table.
2 .... the glasses?   .... in the box.
3 .... the CD?   .... under the book.
4 .... the boys?   .... behind the girls.
5 .... Zoe?   .... next to Brian.
6 .... the apples?   .... in the bag.

5 Write the questions.

1 ..Where's Corky?..................
He's on the table.
2 ....
They're under the small table.
3 ....
They're behind the sofa.
4 ....
She's on the sofa.
5 ....
He's in front of Zoe.
6 ....
They're next to the blue box.
7 ....
He's under the table.
8 ....
They're in the blue box.

6 Play a memory game.

A: Look at the picture in Exercise 5. Ask questions about it.
B: Look at the picture in Exercise 5. Then close your book and answer the questions.

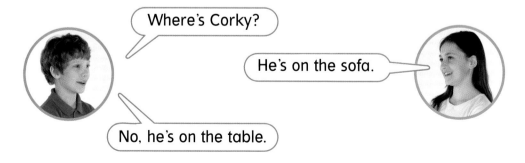

Where's Corky?

He's on the sofa.

No, he's on the table.

Now swap roles.

5 There is, There are

Singular / Plural

Singular			Plural	
Positive	There is There's	a kite.	There are	four ants.
Negative	There is not There isn't	a banana.	There are not There aren't	two sandwiches.
Questions	Is there a cake?		Are there three apples?	
Short answers	Yes, there is. No, there isn't.		Yes, there are. No, there aren't.	

Use the short form when you speak.
You can also use it when you write.

1 Circle the correct word.

1 There **is** / are a kite in the sky.
2 There is / **are** four ants on the grass.
3 There **is** / are a sandwich in the bag.
4 There is / **are** six eggs in the basket.
5 There is / **are** eleven children in the class.
6 There **is** / are a flower on the table.
7 There is / **are** two birds in the tree
8 There **is** / are a chair behind you.

2 Look and answer.

1 Is there a pizza? ....Yes, there is.....
2 Are there four bananas? ....
3 Are there three sandwiches? ....
4 Is there a tomato? ....
5 Are there three oranges? ....
6 Is there a plate? ....
7 Are there four cakes? ....
8 Is there an egg? ....
9 Is there an apple? ....
10 Are there three glasses? ....

5 There is, There are

3 Look and write questions and answers.

1 a bowl?

Is there a bowl?

Yes, there is.

2 two lemons?

Are there two lemons?

No, there aren't.

3 a banana?

....

....

4 two cakes?

....

....

5 a big plate?

....

....

6 a tomato?

....

....

7 two green apples?

....

....

4 Choose and write.

| Are there | Is there an | There are five | Is there a | There are | Is there |

1 .... ant on the grass?

2 .... three pencils in the pencil case?

3 .... cat on the sofa?

4 .... a box in front of the TV?

5 .... three T-shirts in the bag.

6 .... umbrellas in the box.

5 Look and write the correct sentences.

1 There are three pens on the bed.
   No, there aren't. There are five pens on the bed.

2 There's a radio on the desk.
   No, there isn't. There's a TV on the desk.

3 There are four posters on the wall.
   ....

4 There's a box under the table.
   ....

5 There are two T-shirts on the floor.
   ....

6 There's a school bag on the bed.
   ....

6 Ask and answer.

What is there in your friend's room?

Is there a desk?

Are there two chairs?

Yes, there is.

No, there aren't.
There's only one chair!

1 a desk?	4 two windows?	7 a TV?
2 two chairs?	5 a table?	8 six posters?
3 a bed?	6 a bike?	9 a computer?

Now swap roles.

Use your English (Units 3–5)

1 **Point, ask and answer.**

What is this?

It's an alligator.

What's that?

It's a chimp.

1 alligator	3 hamsters	5 puppies	7 iguana
2 chimp	4 goldfish	6 canaries	8 parrot

2 **Circle the correct word(s).**

A: Look at [1] this / these photo!

B: Who is [2] that / those?

A: [3] This / He's my brother. [4] He / That is one year old in this photo.

B: Where [5] he is / is he?

A: He's [6] under / in the kitchen table!

B: He's funny!

3 **Now draw a picture and write a dialogue.**

A: Look at .... photo!

B: Who ....?

A: It's ....
year / years old in this photo.

B: Where ....?

A: ....

B: ....!

34

4 Listen and draw lines.

5 Look at Exercise 4. Ask and answer.

1 *Where's* .... the clock?   *It's on* .... the desk.

2 .... the CDs?   .... the bed.

3 .... plane?   .... bed.

4 .... fish?   .... bowl.

5 .... bag?   .... door.

6 .... skateboard?   .... box.

7 .... books?   .... bed.

8 .... glasses?   .... box.

6 Ask about your partner's room. Then write.

A: Is there a bed?   B: Yes, there is.

A: Where is it?   B: It's next to the window.

A: Are there books?   B: Yes, there are.

A: Where are they?   B: They're in a box, under my bed.

bed	✔	*next to the window*
books	☐	....
pens	☐	....
MP3 player	☐	....
desk	☐	....
TV	☐	....
CDs	☐	....
toys	☐	....

Now you can ...

✔ Ask about and identify things that are near or far.
  – *What's this?*   – *It's a pen.*
  – *What are those?*   – *They are kites.*

✔ Say that something exists.
  There's an apple in the bag.

✔ Say where someone or something is.
  The shoes are under the chair.

6 Possessive adjectives

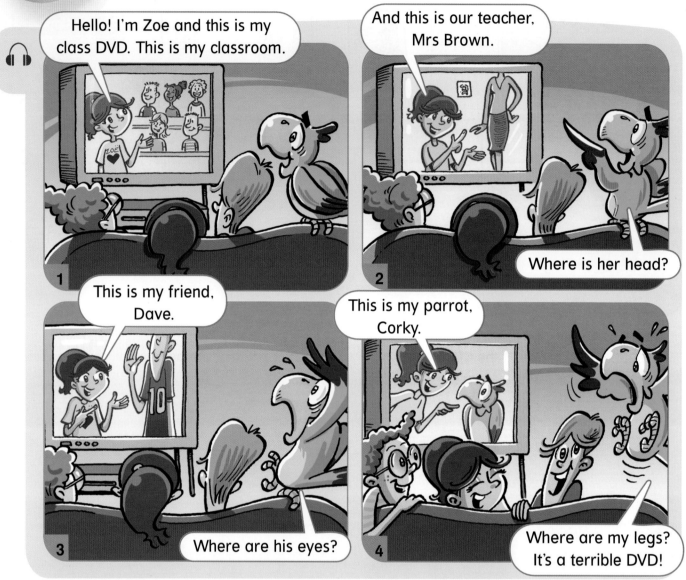

1 Hello! I'm Zoe and this is my class DVD. This is my classroom.

2 And this is our teacher, Mrs Brown.

Where is her head?

3 This is my friend, Dave.

Where are his eyes?

4 This is my parrot, Corky.

Where are my legs? It's a terrible DVD!

Personal pronouns	Possessive adjectives
I	my
you	your
he	his
she	her
it	its
we	our
you	your
they	their

- Always use a noun after a possessive adjective.
  This is my classroom.
  This is our teacher.

1 Circle the correct word.

1

This is my / your new class DVD.

2

That is her / his digicam.

3

That is their / her teacher.

4

Brian is our / their friend.

5

This is my / its cat.

6

That is its / their basket.

2 Look and write *His* or *Her*.

1 ...Her.... cap is blue.
2 .... T-shirt is green.
3 .... jeans are short.
4 .... shoes are brown.
5 .... rucksack is purple.

...His.... cap is green.
.... T-shirt is yellow.
.... jeans are long.
.... shoes are white.
.... rucksack is grey.

3 Put the words in the correct order.

1 is / skateboard / his / This.   This is his skateboard.
2 name / Corky / is / My!   ....
3 classroom / Our / big / is.   ....
4 bag / is / Her / brown.   ....
5 is / dog / white / Their.   ....
6 Its / orange / nose / is.   ....

6 Possessive adjectives

🎧 **4** Read, choose and write.

> your (x2)   our   his   her (x2)   my (x2)

1

Hi! **My** .... name's Brian. What's your name?

Hi! .... name's Vicky.

2

These are .... friends. .... name's Zoe and .... name's Dave.

3

Is that .... class teacher?

Yes, ... name's Miss Taylor.

4

This is .... bus! Goodbye Vicky!

Goodbye Brian!

5 Write questions and answers.

1 this / our classroom?   ✔   Is this our classroom?   Yes, it is.
2 this / your pencil case?   ✔   ....
3 those / his glasses?   ✗   ....
4 that / her schoolbag?   ✗   ....
5 these / their books?   ✔   ....

6 Read and write one word.

Hi! I'm Zoe. I'm in Class 7. This is our classroom.
It's very nice. And this is ¹..our........ class teacher.
²................ name is Mrs Brown. We've got an
art teacher, too. ³................ name is Mr Shaw.
These are ⁴................ classmates. This is Nikki and
this is Diana. They're sisters.

This is ⁵................ pet iguana. It's green and brown.
⁶................ name is Coco.

7 Read. Then draw and write about your friend.

This is my friend. His name is
Dave. He is tall. His hair is short
and his eyes are brown.

This is my friend.
....
....
....
....
....

8 Play a game. Who is it? Take turns.

A: Describe a person in your class.
B: Listen to A. Who is it?

Her hair is long. Her eyes are brown.
Her T-shirt is white. Her shoes are pink.

Yes, it is.

Is it Helen?

Possessive 's

1. Look! This is my scarecrow.

It's very funny!

2. Is this Dave's T-shirt?

Yes, it is. And these are my dad's old trousers.

3. This is Corky's bowl.

And the shoes?

4. Erm … They're your shoes.

Possessive 's	Possessive adjectives
Zoe's scarecrow	**her** scarecrow
Dave's T-shirt	**his** T-shirt
The scarecrow's shoes	**its** shoes

- Zoe's scarecrow is funny.   's = possessive 's.
- Her scarecrow's funny.   's = *is*

- The shoes are Brian's.   's = possessive 's.
- Brian's cross.   's = *is*

1 Write 's.

1 Zoe...'s... scarecrow is funny.
2 Dave........ T-shirt is old.
3 Dad........ trousers are purple.
4 Corky........ bowl is red.
5 The blue shoes are Brian........ .

2 Look, read and write.

1 ...Chloe's... bike is green.   ...Her...... bike is green.
2 .... bike is black.   .... bike is black.
3 .... bag is pink.   .... bag is pink.
4 .... hat is purple.   .... hat is purple.
5 .... inline skates are red.   .... inline skates are red.
6 .... T-shirt is blue.   .... T-shirt is blue.

7 What colour is / are?

Singular	Plural
What colour is Chloe's bike? It's green.	What colour are Katie's inline skates? They're red.

3 Look, read and write.

	Emma	Peter
	🎒	🎒
	🕶	🕶
	👕	👕
	👖	👖

1 What colour is ...*Emma's bag?*...... ...*It's*...... brown.
2 What colour are ...*Emma's sunglasses?*... ...*They're*...... purple.
3 What colour is .... green.
4 .... black.
5 .... red.
6 .... blue.
7 .... grey.
8 .... yellow.

🎧 **4** Read, choose and write.

Corky's Dave's Zoe's my (x2) your

1 This is ...*my*...... chair!

Brian, that's .... chair!

2 Is this .... book, Brian?

No, it isn't. It's ....

3 Hey! Those are .... sunglasses! Dave! Dave!

4 Ooh! Popcorn!

Yes. It's .... popcorn!

5 Find and write.

1 Dave   2 Vicky   3 Brian   4 Zoe   5 Corky   6 Peter

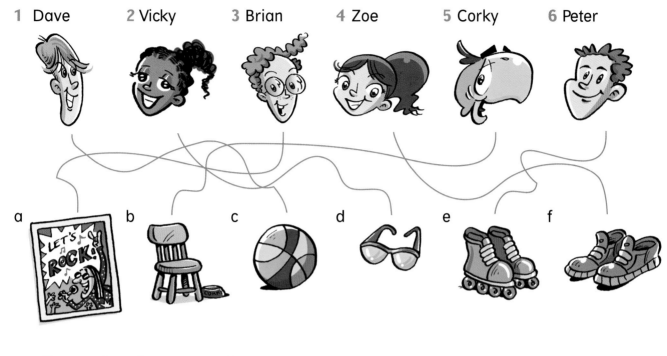

1 *This is Dave's basketball*
2 *These are Vicky's sunglasses*
3 ....

4 ....
5 ....
6 ....

6 Play a game. Can you guess the owner?

This is Jenny's bag.

That's Adam's hat.

have got

have got (negative, question)

Positive		
I You We You They	have got 've got	a chocolate egg. a model plane.

Negative		
I You We You They	have not got haven't got	a chocolate egg. a model plane.

Questions			
Have	I you we you they	got	a chocolate egg? a model plane?

Short answers		
Yes,	I you we	have.
No,	you they	haven't.

1 **Look, choose and write.**

funny noses   a pizza   ~~an ice cream~~   big feet   a green bike

1

I *'ve got an ice cream.*

2 We...

3 You..

4 I...!

5 They..

2 **Write the negative.**

1 They've got a model car.   *They haven't got* a model car.
2 You've got a new bike.   .... a new bike.
3 I've got a red pen.   .... a red pen.
4 We've got an ice cream.   .... an ice cream.
5 They've got a parrot.   .... a parrot.
6 You've got a green kite.   .... a green kite.

3 **Write questions and answers.**

1 they / a watch?
   Have they got a watch?   Yes, they *have.*
2 we / a new teacher?
   ....   No, we ....
3 I / a red nose?
   ....   No, you ....
4 you / a rubber?
   ....   Yes, I ....
5 they / a computer?
   ....   No, they ....

has got negative, question)

Positive			Negative		
He She It	has got 's got	the camera. six legs.	He She It	has not got hasn't got	the camera. six legs.

Questions				Short answers		
Has	he she it	got	the camera? six legs?	Yes, No,	he she it	has. hasn't.

4 Look, read and write.

1 Zoe's got a mouse.
   She hasn't got a mouse. She's got a parrot.
   ....

2 The boy has got two cats.
   ....

3 The girls have got a rabbit.
   ....

4 The woman has got a fish.
   ....

5 The cat has got short fur.
   ....

6 The dogs have got red collars.
   ....

5 Look, read and write.

	a cat	a CD player	a camera
Brian	✔	✗	✔
Zoe	✗	✔	✗

1 *Has Brian got* .... a cat?
   Yes, he has.

2 *Has Zoe got* .... a cat?
   ....

3 .... a CD player?
   ....

4 .... a CD player?
   ....

5 .... a camera?
   ....

6 .... a camera?
   ....

have got, has got (all forms)

6 **Circle the correct word.**

1 I haven't / hasn't got a computer.
2 He've / 's got brown hair.
3 Paula and Simon has / have got new bikes.
4 My dog hasn't / haven't got a long tail.
5 We 've / 's got a cake.
6 A: Has / Have Susan got an i-pod?
  B: Yes, she have / has.
7 A: Has / Have your mum and dad got a digicam?
  B: No, they hasn't / haven't.
8 A: Have / Has you got brothers and sisters?
  B: Yes, I have / has.

7 **Look, read and write.**

1 They've got .... popcorn!

2 .... inline skates.

3 .... a rubber?

4 .... a present for her mum.

5 .... balloons!

6 .... tail?

7 .... a watch.

8 .... new shoes?

8 Read, choose and write.

> got   Have   've got (x2)   haven't got   's got (x2)

Dear Jade,
I ¹ _'ve got_ .... a pet parrot.
His name's Corky.
He ² .... a funny head.
Parrots ³ .... noses.
They ⁴ .... beaks.
Corky ⁵ .... a big beak.
⁶ .... you ⁷ .... a pet?
Love,
Zoe

9 Draw and write.

Write a letter to Zoe about your pet or a friend's pet. Look at the words for help.

> face   ears   nose   tail   legs   fur   cute   funny   pretty   soft

Dear Zoe,
I've got / My friend's got ....
Its name is ....
....
....
....
....
Love,
....

10 Ask and answer. Take turns.

Have you got a pet?

Yes, I have. I've got a cat. / No, I haven't.

1 you / a pet?
2 you / a bike?
3 your friends / bikes?
4 you / posters in your room?

5 your family / a DVD player?
6 your dad / a car?
7 your mum / a digital camera?

9 can

1. Hello, Corky! I'm Danny and I can talk!
   Can you walk?

2. Yes, I can walk and I can jump! Look!
   Yes, but you can't dance!

3. Oh, yes I can! Look!

4. Oh, no!
   Danny can fly, too!

Positive			Negative			Questions			Short answers		
I You He She It We They	can	talk. jump. fly.	I You He She It We They	cannot can't	talk. jump. fly.	Can	I you he she it we they	talk? jump? fly?	Yes, No,	I you he she it we they	can. can't.

50

1 Write *can* or *can't*.

1 He .c.a.n.. play basketball.

2 He .... read.

3 It .... walk.

4 She .... count.

5 They .... fly.

6 He .... swim.

7 They .... sing.

8 She .... ride a bike.

9 It .... jump.

2 Write the correct sentences.

1 Babies can fly.
   Babies can't fly.

2 Ballerinas can't dance.
   Ballerinas can dance.

3 Fish can walk.
   ....

4 Monkeys can't jump.
   ....

5 Teachers can't read.
   ....

6 Teddy bears can run.
   ....

7 Frogs can't swim.
   ....

9   can

🎧 **3**   **Look, read and write.**

1

...Can...... you open the door?

No, I ....

2

Dave, can .... open the door?

He can't .... the door!

3

.... you open it, boys?

..............., we can't!

4

.... you open the door with this key?

CORKY!

4   **Read and write.**

Corky	fly ✔	ride a bike ✗
Zoe	sing ✔	run fast ✔
Brian & Dave	dance ✗	play basketball ✔

1 ...Can........ Corky fly?   Yes, *he can.*...............

2 .... he ride a bike?   No, ...

3 .... Zoe sing?   ....

4 .... she run fast?   ....

5 .... Brian and Dave dance?   ....

6 .... they play basketball?   ....

5   **Look at Exercise 4. Write.**

1 Corky ...*can fly*............... but ...*he can't ride a bike.*...............

2 Zoe .... and ....

3 Brian and Dave .... but ....

6 **Put the questions in the correct order. Write true answers.**

1 you / Can / a / car / drive ?
.....Can you drive a car?........ .....No, I can't.........

2 horse / a / Can / ride / you ?
....

3 basketball / play / Can / you ?
....

4 the / you / play / guitar / Can ?
....

5 run / you / Can / fast ?
....

6 you / Can / swim ?
....

7 **Ask and answer. Complete the chart about your partner.**

Can you ride a bike?

Can you ride a horse?

Yes, I can.

No, I can't.

8 **Tell the class about your partner.**

Rose can ride a bike but she can't ride a horse.

Now swap roles.

Use your English (Units 6–9)

1 **Listen and write T (true) or F (false).**

1 Nick's got a bike. ☐
2 Nick hasn't got a skateboard. ☐
3 Kate can't ride a bike. ☐

4 Kate's bike is green and yellow. ☐
5 Kate's got a cat. ☐
6 Her cat's name is Ollie. ☐

2 **Look, read and correct the sentences.**

1 Sally can't run.
Sally can run.
....

2 Ian can ride a horse.
....

3 Sandra's got a skateboard.
....

4 Sam can walk.
....

5 Ben and Jason can't skate.
....

6 Diana's got a CD player.
....

3 **Look and find. Then write.**

1 *It's Ben's skateboard.*
....

2 ....

3 ....

4 ....

5 ....

6 ....

4 **Circle the correct word.**

A: Is this ¹you / your CD player?

B: No, it isn't. It's ²Peter's / Peters'. ³He / I haven't got a CD player.

A: ⁴You can / Can you ride a horse?

B: No, I ⁵can / can't but I can ride a bike!

A: Is that ⁶Tony's brother / Tony brother's?

B: No, it isn't. Tony ⁷haven't / hasn't got a brother. He's ⁸has / got a sister.

A: ⁹Has / Can Anna swim?

B: ¹⁰Yes / No, she can. She's very good. Can you swim?

A: Yes, I ¹¹am / can.

5 **Do the puzzle. Find the secret word!**

```
                    6        9
                   ┌──┐     ┌──┐
                   │  │     │  │
              5    ├──┤  7  ├──┤
             ┌──┐  │  │ ┌──┐│  │
  1  2  3  4 │  │  │  │ │  ││  │  8
 ┌──┬──┬──┬──┼──┼──┴──┼──┤ └──┼──┐
 │  │  │  │  │  │     │  │    │  │
 ├──┼──┼──┼──┼──┤     ├──┤    ├──┤
 │  │  │  │  │  │     │  │    │  │
 └──┴──┼──┼──┼──┘     └──┼──┘ └──┘
       │  │  │           │
       └──┴──┘           │
                      ┌──┤
                      │  │
                      └──┘
```

1 They … fly.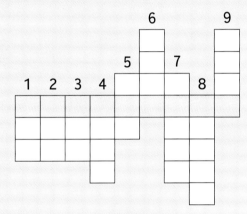

2 This is Zoe's bag. It's … bag.

3 Hi! We are Zoe and Dave.
This is Brian. He is … friend.

4 Dave … swim

5 I've … a BMX bike.

6 Zoe isn't a boy. She is a … .

7

8 It's Sam and Helen's car.
It's … car.

9 A: Have you got a dog?
B: Yes, I … .

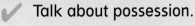

Now you can …

✔ Talk about possession.
My bike is red.   This is John's house.   We've got a dog.

✔ Talk about ability.
I can ride a horse.   Tom can't swim.

10 Imperatives

Is this your new robot?

Yes, it is. Say 'Hello', Robbie!

HELLO!

Say 'Goodbye', Robbie!

GOODBYE!

Turn left, Robbie!

Go to the door! No, stop! Don't go to the door! Come here!

Robbie, sit down, stand up, don't go to the window.

Oh, no!

Positive imperative

Say 'Hello'!
Turn left!
Go to the door!

Negative imperative

Don't go to the door!
Don't turn left!

56

1 Look, choose and write.

stand up   go   ~~come~~   close   open   write   sit down   say

1 ..Come...... here!

2 .... to the door!

3 .... the door!

4 .... the window!

5 ....

6 ....

7 .... your name!

8 .... 'Goodbye'!

2 Put the words in the correct order.

1 window / the / to / Go !   _Go to the window!_ ....

2 book / your / Read !   ....

3 two / Write / names !   ....

4 on / Sit / chair / the !   ....

5 your / Drink / milk !   ....

6 your / Eat / spinach !   ....

3 **Choose and write.**

go open ~~don't sit~~ don't turn don't eat say

1 ....*Don't*............. on this chair!
2 .... to the park!
3 .... my chocolate!
4 .... your books!
5 .... left!
6 .... 'Hello'!

4 **Look, choose and write.**

read (✗) come (✔) sit (✔) ~~close~~ (✔) talk (✔) open (✗) eat (✗)

1

Hello, Zoe.

Please ....*close*......
the door, Dave!

2 Don't .... the window, Dave! I've got a cold!

.... my book, Brian! .... to me!

3

4

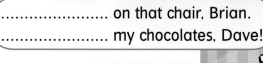

.... on that chair, Brian.
.... my chocolates, Dave!

.... with me, Dave! Goodbye, Zoe. Get well soon!

5

5 Look and write.

School Rules

1 ....Don't talk........... in class.

4 ....

2 .... to your teacher.

5 ....

3 .... sweets.

6 ....

6 Play a game.

A: Give instructions to your partner.
B: Listen to A and follow the instructions.

 Open your mouth!

Count to five.

- open / mouth ✔
- close / eyes ✗
- write / name ✔
- say / 'Goodbye' ✔
- stand up ✗

- count / to five ✔
- sit down ✗
- take off / shoes ✗
- touch / nose ✔
- say / 'Hello' ✗

Now swap roles.

Present simple

I, you, we, they (negative, question)

Can you tell me about your day? It's for my school project.

Yes, of course.

1

I get up at seven o'clock.

2

I have breakfast. I drink a glass of milk.

3

I go to school.

4

Do you walk to school?

No, I don't. My friends and I take the bus.

5

In the evening I do my homework.

6

Positive		
I You We They	get up have breakfast do homework	at 7 o'clock. every day. in the evening.

Negative			
I You We They	do not don't	get up have breakfast do homework	at 7 o'clock. every day. in the evening.

Questions			
Do	I you we they	get up have breakfast do homework	at 7 o'clock? every day? in the evening

Short answers		
Yes,	I you we they	do.
No,		don't.

We use the present simple to talk about things we do regularly.

1 **Write.**

Positive ✔   **Negative** ✗

1   I drink milk.   I _don't drink_ tea.
2   We play basketball.   We _don't play_ football.
3   You take the bus to school.   You .... a taxi.
4   They read comics.   They .... books.
5   We eat bananas.   We .... strawberries.
6   I get up at eight o'clock.   I .... at seven oclock.

2 **Write questions and answers.**

1   you / get up   _Do you get up_ .... at seven o'clock?   Yes, I _do._ ....
2   they / drink   .... juice in the morning?   No, they ....
3   you / like   .... cherries?   No, I ....
4   they / take   .... the bus every day?   Yes, they ....
5   you / do your homework ....   Yes, I ....
    in the evening?

3 **Look, read and write.**

1

I .... my teeth every morning.

brush ✔

2

We .... swimming every Sunday

go ✔

3

They .... like spinach!

like ✗

4

.... you .... football every Saturday?

play **?**

5

.... you .... TV every day?

watch **?**

6

We .... pizza every day!

eat ✗

he, she, it (negative, question)

1

2

3

4

Positive	
He She It	lik**es** chocolate cake. run**s** fast.

Negative		
He She It	does not doesn't	like chocolate cake. run fast.

Questions		
Does	he she it	like chocolate cake? run fast?

Short answers		
Yes,	he she it	does.
No,		doesn't.

We use the present simple to talk about facts.

Spelling rules: 3rd person singular

Verb + -s		Verb + -es	
• like	➡ like**s**	• do	➡ do**es**
• play	➡ play**s**	• go	➡ go**es**
• sit	➡ sit**s**	• wash	➡ wash**es**
		• watch	➡ watch**es**

4 Choose and write.

~~like~~ eat play buy take drink

Positive ✔

1 Vicky ...*likes*... chocolate cake.
2 The cat .... milk.
3 Brian .... books.
4 Dave .... football.
5 Zoe .... the bus to school.
6 Corky .... ice cream.

Negative ✗

She ...*doesn't like*... spinach.
It .... orange juice.
He .... comics.
He .... tennis.
She .... a taxi.
He .... tomatoes.

5 Read and write.

Zoe
Friday – play volleyball
Saturday – get up at eleven o'clock
Sunday – go to the park

Brian
Friday – watch TV
Saturday – wash Dad's car
Sunday – do my homework

1 Zoe ...*plays volleyball*... every Friday.
2 She .... at eleven o'clock every Saturday.
3 She .... to the park every Sunday.

4 Brian .... TV every Friday.
5 He .... his dad's car every Saturday.
6 He .... his homework every Sunday.

> They do these things every weekend.

6 Look at Exercise 5. Write questions and and answers.

1 ...*Does*... Zoe ...*play volleyball*... every Friday?
   Yes, she does.
2 .... she .... at seven o'clock every Saturday?
   No, she doesn't. She gets up at eleven o'clock.
3 .... to the cinema every Sunday?
   ....
4 .... Brian .... TV every Friday?
   ....
5 .... he .... his Dad's car every Sunday?
   ....
6 .... he .... his homework every Saturday?
   ....

11 All forms

🎧 **7** Look, read and write.

I _like_ .... Saturdays. I .... at eleven o'clock. I .... to school.

1 like ✔ get up ✔ go ✗

We .... in the garden. We .... TV. We .... for school!

2 play ✔ watch ✔ study ✗

We .... to the park. Dave .... basketball. Brian .... his bike.

3 go ✔ play ✔ ride ✔

.... Saturdays, Corky?

4 like ?

Yes, I do. But today is Friday!

🎧 **8** Write *do, does, don't* or *doesn't*.

Vicky: [1] _Do_ .... you like ice cream?

Zoe: Yes, I [2] ....

Vicky: [3] .... Corky like ice cream, too?

Zoe: Yes, he [4] .... And he likes pizza. But he [5] .... like spinach.

Vicky: [6] .... you and your friends come to the park every weekend?

Zoe: Yes, we [7] .... Dave and I play basketball. Brian reads books. [8] .... you play basketball at the weekend?

Vicky: No, I [9] .... But I play tennis every Saturday.

Zoe: [10] .... your mum and dad play tennis?

Vicky: No, they [11] .... They [12] .... like sport.

64

9 **Read, choose and write.**

watch   have   ~~get up~~   like   go   play   listen   do   don't like

My Saturday

I ¹ ..get up.............. at ten o'clock. I ² ....
breakfast with my mum and dad and my brother, Seb.
    After breakfast, my brother and I ³ ....
to music. He ⁴ .... The Emperor Kings but I
⁵ .... them. They're very bad.
    In the afternoon I ⁶ .... to the park
with my friends. We ⁷ .... football or
basketball.
    In the evening I ⁸ .... DVDs. My brother
⁹ .... his homework.

10 **Write about your Saturday.**

I get up at ....
After breakfast ....
....
In the afternoon ....
....
In the evening ....
....

11 **Look at Exercise 10. Ask and answer.**

Do you get up at seven o'clock?

No, I don't. I get up at nine o'clock.

What do you do after breakfast?

I go swimming.

Now swap roles.

12 **Tell the class about your partner.**

Rose gets up at nine o'clock.
After breakfast she goes swimming.

12 *have / has*

Positive	
I / You / We / They	have a pen.
He / She / It	has a present.

Negative			
I / You / We / They	do not don't	have	a pen.
He / She / It	does not doesn't		a present.

Questions		
Do I / you / we / they	have	a pen?
Does he / she / it		a present?

Short answers			
Yes, / No,	I / you / we / they	do. / don't.
	he / she / it	does. / doesn't

- *Have* and *have got* mean the same.

have	*have got*
I have a pen.	*I've got a pen.*
***Do** you **have** a pen? Yes, I **do**.*	***Have** you **got** a pen? Yes, I **have**.*

1 Look and write *have* or *has*.

1

He ...*has*... a little sister.

2

She .... a goldfish.

3

They .... a red kite.

4

It .... a long tail.

5

We .... a picnic basket.

6

I .... a new bike.

2 Look at Exercise 1. Write questions and answers.

1 ...*Does*... Dave ...*have*... a little brother?   No, ...*he doesn't.*...

2 .... Zoe .... a goldfish?   Yes, ...

3 .... Dave and Brian .... a model plane ?   ....

4 .... the alligator .... a long tail?   ....

5 .... Zoe, Dave and Brian .... a picnic basket?   ....

6 .... Brian .... a new bike?   ....

3   **Look. Write the correct sentences.**

1   Zoe has red hair.   *She doesn't have red hair. She has brown hair.*
2   Brian has small glasses.   ....
3   Dave and Brian have long hair. ....
4   Corky has a small beak.   ....
5   Vicky has a green dress.   ....
6   The frogs have short legs.   ....

4   **Put the words in the correct order. Write true answers.**

1   you / Do / red / hair / have?
    Do you have red hair? ....   *Yes, I do. / No, I don't.*

2   a bike / best friend / Does / have / your?
    ....

3   we / teacher / have / Do / a new ?
    ....

4   beaks / people / Do / have ?
    ....

5   have / you / a computer / Do ?
    ....

6   a frog / Does / have / a tail ?
    ....

5 **Choose and write.**

is   's (x2)   Do   doesn't   has (x2)   comes   play

Dear Lisa,

My teacher's name is Mrs Jones. She [1] ...ˢ........... young and pretty. Here [2] .... a photo! She [3] .... long, brown hair and green eyes. She [4] .... have a big car but she [5] .... a huge dog. His name [6] .... Bobby. Every Friday Bobby [7] .... to our school and we [8] .... with him. [9] .... you have a photo of your teacher?

Love,

Zoe

6 **Write about your teacher. Answer the questions**

1 What is your teacher's name?
2 Does your teacher have long or short hair?
3 Does your teacher have brown, blue or green eyes?
4 Does your teacher have a car?
5 Does your teacher have a pet?

My teacher's name is ....
She / he has ....
....
....
....

7 **Play a game.**

A: Think of a person in the class.
B: Guess the person.

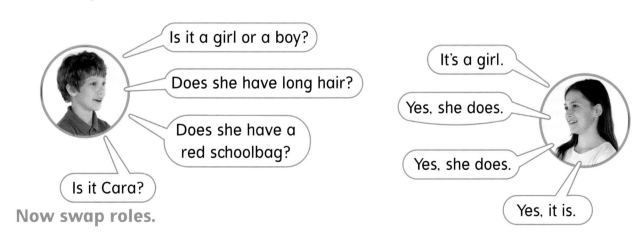

Is it a girl or a boy?

Does she have long hair?

Does she have a red schoolbag?

Is it Cara?

It's a girl.

Yes, she does.

Yes, she does.

Yes, it is.

Now swap roles.

Use your English (Units 10–12)

🎧 **1** **Listen and tick ✔.**

1 A Open it. ☐
　 B Eat it. ☐

2 A Don't turn left. ☐
　 B Don't sit on it! ☐

3 A Drink it. ☐
　 B Read it. ☐

4 A Watch TV. ☐
　 B Go to bed! ☐

5 A Don't eat it! ☐
　 B Say 'Hello'. ☐

6 A Run to the door! ☐
　 B Don't talk! ☐

2 **Circle the correct word.**

1 I get up / gets up at seven o'clock every day.
2 Peter walk / walks to school in the morning.
3 We play / plays basketball every Sunday.
4 They don't / doesn't have homework every day.
5 My mum don't / doesn't like tennis.
6 Does / Do Corky like ice cream?
7 Do your friends go / goes swimming every Friday?
8 Does / Do you have a parrot?

3 **Write questions.**

1 you / get up / six o'clock
2 you / walk / to school ?
3 your dad / drive / to work ?
4 you / have / homework / every day ?
5 your mum / watch / TV ?
6 you / have / brother or sister ?
7 your best friend / have / a pet ?
8 you / go to bed / nine o'clock?

Do you get up at six o'clock?
Do you walk to school?
....
....
....
....
....
....

4 **Ask and answer the questions in Exercise 3.**

Do you get up at six o'clock?

No, I don't. I get up at eight o'clock

5 **Choose and write.**

drinks   has (x3)   doesn't   runs   eats   six   green

PET MONSTER COMPETITION!

Write about your pet monster!

My pet monster ¹..has....... a big, red head and three ² .... eyes. It ³............... four legs and ⁴............... arms. It ⁵............... have big ears but it ⁶............... a big nose.

Its legs are short but it ⁷............... fast. It ⁸............... rubbers, pencils and brushes. It ⁹............... tomato juice.

Brian,

6 **Choose and write.**

1 ...Read................... this book. It's very funny!
   a Write   b Read   c Watch

2 .... TV every day.
   a We don't watch   b Do we watch   c Don't we watch

3 Helen and Chris .... a red car.
   a doesn't have   b don't have   c haven't

4 .... eat fish?
   a You do   b Does they   c Does he

5 .... the window, please. I'm cold.
   a Close   b Open   c Stop

6 .... big windows?
   a Has your school   b Your school has   c Does your school have

Now you can ...

✔ Give and understand instructions.
Turn right here.
Don't open the window.
✔ Talk about routines or things you do regularly.
I drink milk every day.
Maria doesn't get up early.

Prepositions of time, *when*

Prepositions of time

Prepositions of time (1)

at + time:	at ten o'clock / half past eleven
on + days:	on Saturday / Sunday
in + months:	in January / April
in + seasons:	in the summer / winter

1 Look and write.

1 Zoe gets up .....at seven o'clock.....................

2 Brian has breakfast .....at half past seven.........

3 School starts ....

4 The children have lunch ....

5 They go home ....

6 Corky goes to bed ....

2 Choose and write.

July October January August November April February May

Spring	Summer	Autumn	Winter

3 Put the days of the week in the correct order.

Friday Tuesday Sunday Wednesday Monday Saturday Thursday

Monday
....

....

4 Write *in* or *on*.

1 The school party is .... Friday.
2 School finishes .... July.
3 We go to the beach .... the summer.
4 The football match is .... Saturday.
5 My family goes on holiday .... August.
6 It's cold .... the winter.

5 **Read, draw lines and match.**

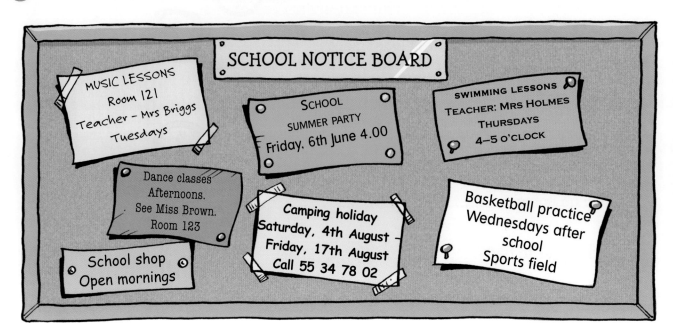

1 When are the swimming lessons?   a In the afternoons.
2 When is the school summer party?   b At four o'clock.
3 What time does the party start?   c On Thursdays.
4 When are the dance classes?   d On Friday, 6th June.

Prepositions of time (2)

on + days and dates	on Tuesday, 10th April
in + parts of the day	in the morning / afternoon / evening

Look!

on Tuesdays = every Tuesday
in the afternoons = every afternoon

When? What time?

When is your birthday?	On the 11th of June.
When do you get up? What time …?	At 7 o'clock.

We say 'on the tenth of April'.

6 **Look at Exercise 5. Write short answers.**

1 When is the school shop open?   ....
2 When does the camping holiday start? ....
3 When are the music lessons?   ....
4 When is basketball practice?   ....

7 Write about Zoe.

1 Tuesdays / have a music lesson
   On Tuesdays she has a music lesson.

2 Wednesdays / play basketball
   ....

3 Thursdays / swimming lesson
   ....

4 Fridays / play volleyball
   ....

5 Saturdays / go to the park
   ....

8 Look, read and write.

1 A: .....*When*..... is your birthday?
  B: ...*On*...... the fifth of May.

2 A: .... is Vicky's party?
  B: .... Saturday.

3 A: .... time does the party start?
  B: .... six o'clock.

4 A: .... do you do your homework?
  B: .... the afternoon, after school.

5 A: .... does your school close?
  B: .... June.

6 A: .... do you go to the cinema?
  B: .... Saturdays.

9 Ask and answer. Take turns.

When is your birthday?

On the 25th of June.

1 be / your birthday?
2 you / get up?
3 you / have English lessons?
4 you / watch TV?

5 you / do your homework?
6 you / go to bed?
7 you / go on holiday?

14 Question words

Question words	
Who is (Who's) this?	It's my friend.
What is (What's) your address?	It's 20 Green Street.
What colour is (What colour's) your bike?	It's red.
What time do you get up?	I get up at seven o'clock.
Where is (Where's) your house?	It's near the school.
When is (When's) your birthday?	It's on the 15th of May.
How are you?	I'm fine.
How old is (How old's) Anna?	She's nine.
How many brothers has she got?	She's got one brother.

1 Draw lines and match.

1 When's Tom's birthday?
2 How are you?
3 How old are you?
4 Who's this?
5 How many pens have you got?
6 Where's the cake?
7 What are these?
8 Where do you live?
9 What's your favourite food?
10 What colour's your bag?

a I'm ten.
b It's my brother, Nick.
c I've got twelve.
d They're strawberries.
e It's on the 14th of September.
f At 15 Porthall Gardens.
g Chocolate.
h It's purple
i It's on the table.
j I'm fine.

2 Circle the correct word(s).

1

What's / Who's that?

It's my new phone.

2

How many / How old sisters have you got?

I've got one sister.

3

Who's / What's this?

She's my friend, Vicky.

4

When's / How old's Vicky?

She's ten.

5

Who / How are you?

I'm fine, thanks.

6

How's / Where's Zoe?

I don't know.

77

Question words

🎧 **3** **Look, choose and write.**

How old   What time   ~~How~~   Who   Where

It's six o'clock on Saturday.

How .... are you, Corky?

I'm not very well.

............'s Zoe?

She's at Anna's house.

............'s Anna?

She's Zoe's new friend.

.... is Anna?

She's nine. It's her birthday today. They're at Anna's party and I'm here!

.... does the party finish?

Poor Corky!

I don't know!

4 **Read the answers. Then write the questions.**

1 .... that?   It's Helen. She's my friend.
2 .... posters
   ....?   I've got three posters.
3 .... the apples?   They're on the table.
4 .... Peter's birthday?   It's on the 12th of November.
5 .... the party start?   It starts at half past seven.
6 .... your friend?   She isn't very well.

5 Put the words in the correct order. Write true answers.

1 are / old / you / How ?

.... I'm ....

2 your / When's / birthday ?

....

3 do / Where / live / you ?

....

4 food / What's / favourite / your ?

....

5 favourite / your / singer / Who's ?

....

6 CDs / got / How many / you / have ?

....

6 Look at Exercise 5. Ask and answer. Write.

How old are you?   I'm nine.

Name: Peter ....
Age: ....
Birthday: ....
Address: ....
Favourite food: ....
Favourite singer: ....
Number of CDs: ....

7 Write about your friend.

My friend Peter .... is ....
birthday ....
His address ....
....
....
....
....

Present continuous

I, we, you, they (question, negative)

I'm singing on TV!

Dave! You aren't playing basketball! You're sewing!

We're dancing!

Hmm?

They're eating spinach! Am I dreaming?

Positive		
I	am / 'm	singing. playing.
We You They	are / 're	

Negative		
I	am not / 'm not	singing. playing.
We You They	are not / aren't	

We use the present continuous for something that is happening at this moment.

Questions		
Am	I	singing? dancing?
Are	we you they	

Short answers		
Yes,	I	am.
No,		am not / 'm not.
Yes,	we you they	are
No,		are not / 're not.

1 **Write.**

Positive ✔

Negative ✗

1 (read)
   I...**'m reading**......... a book.

(watch)
   I...**'m not watching**... TV.

2 (do)
   We............................ our homework.

(play)
   We............................ basketball.

3 (eat)
   They............................ ice cream.

(drink)
   They............................ orange juice.

4 (talk)
   You............................ to your friend.

(listen)
   You............................ to me.

5 (fly)
   You............................

(walk)
   You............................

2 **What's happening now? Write true answers.**

1 Are we studying English? .....**Yes, we are.**.........
2 Are you wearing a T-shirt? ....
3 Are your friends playing basketball? ....
4 Are we looking at our books? ....
5 Are your mum and dad working? ....
6 Are you listening to your teacher? ....

3 **Look, read and write.**

It's Saturday afternoon ...

Where are Zoe, Dave and Brian?
What ...**are**... they ...**doing**...?

.... you .... out?

Hey! Wait!
You..................... very fast!

1 do **?**

2 go **?**

3 walk ✔

They .... to me!

Sorry, Corky. We.....................
to the cinema and we're late!

They..................... with me! I..................... home!

4 listen ✗

5 go ✔

6 play ✗, go ✔

Positive		
He She It	is 's	reading a magazine. sleeping.

Negative		
He She It	is not isn't	reading a magazine. sleeping.

Questions		
Is	he she it	reading a magazine? sleeping?

Short answers		
Yes,	he she	is.
No,	it	isn't.

Questions with question words		
What		she doing?
Where	is	he going?
Who		singing?

4 Look and write.

1 (read/listen to)
Brian *isn't reading* a magazine. He *'s listening to* music.

2 (eat/drink)
Corky .... chocolate. He........................... milk.

3 (play/fly)
Dave .... basketball. He........................... a model plane.

4 (talk/read)
Anna .... to Brian. She........................... a book.

5 (sleep/climb)
The cat .... under the tree. It........................... the tree.

5 Look at the picture in Exercise 4. Write questions and answers.

1 Corky / sleep?   Is *Corky sleeping* ? No, *he isn't.*
2 Zoe / look at the birds? Is ....? Yes, ...
3 the cat / drink milk?   ....? ....
4 Brian / listen to music? ....? ....
5 Anna / do her homework?   ....? ....
6 Vicky / play basketball? ....? ....

6 Read the answers. Then write the questions.

1 Where *are they playing* ? They're playing in the park.
2 Who ....? Brian's listening to music.
3 What ....? Dave's wearing jeans and a T-shirt.
4 Who ....? Vicky is playing tennis.
5 What ....? Corky's drinking milk.
6 Where ....? They're going home now.

Spelling rules: verb + *-ing*

Verbs that end in *-e*			Verbs that end in a vowel + consonant:		
dance	→ ∅	→ dancing	swim	→ mm →	swimming
come	→ ∅	→ coming	run	→ nn →	running
close	→ ∅	→ closing	stop	→ pp →	stopping
ride	→ ∅	→ riding	sit	→ tt →	sitting
write	→ ∅	→ writing			

Look!

sleep → sleeping

Be careful with the spelling!

7   Look, read and write.

Quiet, Corky! We*'re doing* our homework!

LA! LA! LA!

1   do ✔

.... he ....?

No, he ....
He....................!

2   jump ?, dance ✔

I.................... chocolate! Look, Corky! Yummy!

Chocolate! Wait! I....................!

3   eat ✔, come ✔

.... you .... the window?

Yes! He .... now! We can do our homework.

4   close ?, sing ✗

8 Write the *-ing* forms.

> drive   sing   run   watch   sit   write   fly   ride   swim

play + -ing = playing	dance + -ing = dancing	stop + -ing = stopping
1	4	7 ....
2	5	8 ....
3	6	9 ....

9 Look, read and write.

1 she / drive / her new car ✔   2 we / run ✗   3 they / write / a test ✔

4 you / sleep ?   5 he / swim ?   6 they / study ✗

10 Play a memory game.

A: Look at the picture in Exercise 4. Ask questions about it.
B: Look at the picture in Exercise 4. Then close your book and answer the questions.

What's Brian doing?

Yes, that's right.

He's listening to music.

Now swap roles.

Use your English (Units 13–15)

🎧 **1** **Listen and match.**

1 Tom goes ski-ing   a   in August.
2 Betty's birthday is   b   at half past two.
3 The football match is   c   in the morning.
4 Samantha usually has lunch   d   in the winter.
5 In Australia it isn't very cold   e   in June.
6 David never watches TV   f   on the 10th of June.

2 **Read. Then write the questions**

Ryan is a student. He is ten years old and he lives in London. He's got two brothers. He likes music and films. He has piano lessons on Wednesdays and he always goes to the cinema on Fridays.

His best friend is Nick. He is eleven years old. He hasn't got a brother or a sister but he's got a cat, three hamsters and a parrot. Nick's house is next to Ryan's. In the morning, they walk to school together.

1 _How old is Ryan?_   Ten.
2 _Where does he live?_   In London.
3 .... like?   Music and films.
4 .... to the cinema?   On Fridays.
5 .... Nick?   Ryan's best friend.
6 .... Nick got?   Five.
7 .... go to school?   They walk.

3 **Ask and answer.**

How old are you?   I'm ten years old.

1 How old?   4 When / go out with / friends?
2 Where / live?   5 Where / go?
3 What / like?   6 Who / favourite pop star?

4 **Look, choose and write.**

play   eat   sing   swim   drink   read   sleep   run

1 A young man ....
2 Two boys .... volleyball.
3 A woman .... a magazine.
4 The brown dog ....

5 Two girls .... lemonade.
6 A boy .... a sandwich.
7 The white dog ....
8 A bird ....

5 **Do the puzzle. Find a secret message from Zoe, Brian, Dave & Corky!**

1 The young man in Exercise 4 is … .
2 The month after May.
3 A: … do you go to the park?
   B: On Saturdays.
4 The boys in Exercise 4 are … volleyball.
5 The party is … the 25th of August.
6 My birthday is … July.
7 I get up … half past seven.
8 The … in Exercise 4 is eating.
9 A: …'s this? B: It's my new CD player.
10 A: … are my books? B: They're on the desk.

Unit 1

Articles: *a*/*an*

- We use *a* with words that begin with a consonant: b c d f g h j k l m n p q r s t v w x y z
  a bag   *a cat*   *a dog*   *a frog*   *a kite*   *a pen*   *a rubber*   *a teacher*   *a window*
  a zebra
- We use *an* with words that begin with a vowel: a e i o u
  an alligator   *an elephant*   *an iguana*   *an ostrich*   *an umbrella*

Spelling rules for regular plural nouns

- To make the plural of most nouns, we add *-s* at the end of the word:
  a book ⟶ *two books*
  a cake ⟶ *four cakes*
  an orange ⟶ *three oranges*
- To make the plural of nouns that end in *-s*, *-ss*, *-sh*, *-ch*, *-x* and *-o*, we add *-es* at the end of the word:

a bus ⟶ *two buses*	*a witch* ⟶ *three witches*
a dress ⟶ *three dresses*	*a fox* ⟶ *two foxes*
a brush ⟶ *four brushes*	*a tomato* ⟶ *six tomatoes*

- To make the plural of nouns that end in consonant + *-y*, we change *-y* to *-i* and add *-es*:
  a baby ⟶ *two babies*
  a cherry ⟶ *four cherries*
  a strawberry *two strawberries*
- To make the plural of nouns that end in vowel + *-y* , we just add *-s* at the end of the word:
  a toy ⟶ *four toys*
  a monkey ⟶ *two monkeys*

Spelling rules for irregular plural nouns

- Some nouns do not add *-s*, *-es* or *-ies* to make the plural. They change in different ways:

a child ⟶ *two children*	*a tooth* ⟶ *three teeth*
a man ⟶ *four men*	*a foot* ⟶ *two feet*
a woman ⟶ *two women*	*a mouse* ⟶ *five mice*

- Some nouns do not change at all in the plural:
  a sheep ⟶ *three sheep*
  a fish ⟶ *two fish*

Unit 2

be: positive, negative

Positive		Negative	
Long form	**Short form**	**Long form**	**Short form**
I am	I'm	I am not	I'm not
You are	You're	You are not	You aren't
He is / She is / It is	He's / She's / It's	He / She / It is not	He / She / It isn't
We are	We're	We are not	We aren't
You are	You're	You are not	You aren't
They are	They're	They are not	They aren't

I am a ballerina. → I'm a ballerina.   We are pupils. → We're pupils.   He is not tall. → He isn't tall.

be: questions, short answers

Questions	Short answers	
	Positive	**Negative**
Am I?	Yes, you are.	No, you aren't.
Are you?	Yes, I am.	No, I'm not.
Is he / she / it?	Yes, he / she / it is.	No, he / she / it isn't.
Are we	Yes, you are.	No, you aren't.
Are you?	Yes, we are.	No, we aren't.
Are they?	Yes, they are.	No, they aren't.

Am I a bird?   Yes, you are. / No, you aren't.

Look!

To make a question, we put the verb first:
I am a girl. → *Am* I a girl?

Unit 8

have got: positive, negative

Positive		Negative	
Long form	**Short form**	**Long form**	**Short form**
I have got	I've got	I have not got	I haven't got
You have got	You've got	You have not got	You haven't got
He has got	He's got	He has not got	He hasn't got
She has got	She's got	She has not got	She hasn't got
It has got	It's got	It has not got	It hasn't got
We have got	We've got	We have not got	We haven't got
You have got	You've got	You have not got	You haven't got
They have got	They've got	They have not got	They haven't got

I have got a red pen. → I've got a red pen.   She has not got a parrot. → She hasn't got a parrot.

have got: questions, short answers

Questions	Short answers	
	Positive	Negative
Have I got?	Yes, you have.	No, you haven't.
Have you got?	Yes, I have.	No, I haven't.
Has he / she / it got?	Yes, he / she / it has.	No, he / she / it hasn't.
Have we got?	Yes, you have.	No, you haven't.
Have you got?	Yes, we have.	No, we haven't.
Have they got?	Yes, they have.	No, they haven't.

Have they got a kite?   Yes, they have. / No, they haven't.

> **Look!**
> To make a question, we put the subject between *have* and *got*:
> **You** have got a bike.
> → Have **you** got a bike?
> **Peter** has got a brother.
> → Has **Peter** got a brother?

Unit 9

can

Positive	Negative	Questions	Short answers	
			Positive	Negative
I can	I can't	Can I?	Yes, you can.	No, you can't.
You can	You can't	Can you?	Yes, I can.	No, I can't.
He can	He can't	Can he?	Yes, he can.	No, he can't.
She can	She can't	Can she?	Yes, she can.	No, she can't.
It can	It can't	Can it?	Yes, it can.	No, it can't.
We can	We can't	Can we?	Yes, you can.	No, you can't.
You can	You can't	Can you?	Yes, we can.	No, we can't.
They can	They can't	Can they?	Yes, they can.	No, they can't.

I can play basketball.   Can she sing? Yes, she can. / No, she can't.

> **Look!**
> To make a question, we put the verb first:
> He **can** swim.
> → **Can** he swim?

Unit 11

Present simple: positive, negative

Positive	Negative	
	Long form	Short form
I eat	I do not eat	I don't eat
You eat	You do not eat	You don't eat
He / She / It eats	He / She / It does not eat	He / She / It doesn't eat
We eat	We do not eat	We don't eat
You eat	You do not eat	You don't eat
They eat	They do not eat	They don't eat

I go to school every day.   My brother plays basketball every Saturday.

> **Look!**
> We add -*s* to the third person *He, She, It*:
> I walk to school every day.
> He / My brother walk**s** to school every day.

Present simple: questions, short answers

Questions	Short answers	
	Positive	**Negative**
Do I eat?	Yes, you do.	No, you don't.
Do you eat?	Yes, I do.	No, I don't.
Does he / she / it eat?	Yes, he / she / it does.	No, he / she / it doesn't.
Do we eat?	Yes, you do.	No, you don't.
Do you eat?	Yes, we do.	No, we don't.
Do they eat?	Yes, they do.	No, they don't.
Do you like pizza? Yes, I do. / No, I don't.		

Look!

To make a question, we put the subject between the auxiliary verb *do* or *does* and the main verb:
I like chocolate cake. → ***Do you like*** *chocolate cake?* ***Does Zoe like*** *chocolate cake?*

Spelling rules for the third person singular (*he*, *she*, *it*)

- To make the third person singular (*he*, *she*, *it*) of most verbs, we add -*s*:
  like → *like**s***
  play → *play**s***
  sit → *sit**s***
- We add –*es* to verbs that end in -*o*, -*s*, -*ch*, -*ss*, -*sh* or -*x*:
  do → *do**es***
  go → *go**es***
  watch → *watch**es***
  wash → *wash**es***
  *I **like** ice cream. He **likes** pizza.*
  *We **play** football every Saturday. She **plays** tennis.*
  *I **go** home at three o'clock. He **goes** home at four o'clock.*

91

Unit 12

have / has: positive, negative

Positive	Negative	
	Long form	Short form
I have	I do not have	I don't have
You have	You do not have	You don't have
He / She / It has	He / She / It does not have	He / She / It doesn't have
We have	We do not have	We don't have
You have	You do not have	You don't have
They have	They do not have	They don't have

I have two sisters.   My brother has a bike.   We don't have a cat.

have / has: questions, short answers

Questions	Short answers	
	Positive	Negative
Do I have?	Yes, you do.	No, you don't.
Do you have?	Yes, I do.	No, I don't.
Does he / she / it have?	Yes, he / she / it does.	No, he / she / it doesn't.
Do we have?	Yes, you do.	No, you don't.
Do you have?	Yes, we do.	No, we don't.
Do they have?	Yes, they do.	No, they don't.

Do you have red hair?   Yes, I do. / No, I don't.

Unit 15

Present continuous: positive, negative

Positive	Negative	
	Long form	Short form
I am singing	I am not singing	I'm not singing
You are singing	You are not singing	You aren't singing
He / She / It is singing	He / She / It is not singing	He / She / It isn't singing
We are singing	We are not singing	We aren't singing
You are singing	You are not singing	You aren't singing
They are singing	They are not singing	They aren't singing

Present continuous: questions, short answers

Questions	Short answers	
	Positive	**Negative**
Am I singing?	Yes, you are.	No, you aren't.
Are you singing?	Yes, I am.	No, I'm not.
Is he / she / it singing?	Yes, he / she / it is.	No, he / she / it isn't.
Are we singing?	Yes, you are.	No, you aren't.
Are you singing?	Yes, we are.	No, we aren't.
Are they singing?	Yes, they are.	No, they aren't.

Look!

To make a question, we put *Am / Is / Are* first, then the subject, then the *-ing* verb:
He is watching TV. → *Is he watching TV?*

Spelling rules for verbs + *-ing*

- To make the present continuous of most verbs, we add *-ing* to the end of the verb:
  do → *doing*
  eat → *eating*
  read → *reading*
  sleep → *sleeping*
  talk → *talking*
- When the verb ends in *-e*, we drop the *-e* and add *-ing*.
  come → *coming*
  dance → *dancing*
  write → *writing*
- When the verb ends in a consonant + vowel + consonant, we double the consonant and add *-ing*:
  swim → *swimming*
  run → *running*
  stop → *stopping*
  sit → *sitting*
- When the final consonant is *-w*, *-x* or *-y*, we do not double it:
  grow → *growing*
  fix → *fixing*
  play → *playing*
  study → *studying*

Word list

Unit 1

alligator
ant
apple
baby
bag
ball
bee
book
box
boy
brush
bus
cake
cat
cherry
child
desk
dress
egg
elephant
eye
fish
foot
fox
friend
frog
girl
glass
hat
igloo
iguana
kite
man
monkey
mouse
octopus
orange
ostrich
pen
potato
rubber
sheep
strawberry
teacher
tomato
tooth
toy

tree
umbrella
watch
window
witch
woman
zebra

Unit 2

bad
ballerina
big
bird
black
CD
clever
cowboy
funny
good
grey
happy
hungry
mad
new
panda
parrot
plane
pretty
pupil
sad
short
silly
singer
small
tall
terrible
turn
white

Unit 3

bear
car
chair
clock
dog
door
horse
pencil

photo
picture

Unit 4

bed
blue
house
park
school
sofa
table
TV
vase

Unit 5

banana
basket
bike
bowl
class
cloud
computer
floor
flower
grass
green
pizza
plate
radio
room
sandwich
sky
wall

Unit 6

brown
classroom
digicam
DVD
hair
head
long
nose
pink
purple
rucksack
skateboard

tail
T-shirt
video
yellow

Unit 7

old
popcorn
red
scarecrow
trousers

Unit 8

brother
camera
chocolate
cute
face
fur
ice cream
i-pod
model
pet
player
sister
smile
soft
surprise

Unit 9

count
dance
drive
fast
fly
guitar
jump
look
open
play basketball / tennis etc.
read
ride a bike
ride a horse
run
swim
talk
walk

Unit 10

close
come
drink
eat
listen
milk
mouth
robot
say
sit down
spinach
stand up
take off
touch
turn left
turn right
write

Unit 11

football
garden
get up
homework
lemonade
like
naughty
project
study
swimming
taxi
teeth
tennis
volleyball

Unit 12

beak
goldfish
picnic
present
ribbon

Unit 13

afternoon
Autumn
beach

breakfast
camping
evening
morning
Spring
Summer
what time
when
Winter

Unit 14

(not) well
address
how many
how old
what
where
who

Unit 15

bored
dream
late
sew

Pearson Education Limited
Edinburgh Gate
Harlow
Essex CM20 2JE
England
and Associated Companies throughout the world.

www.longman.com

First Published in 2001
This edition 2008

Student Book ISBN: 978-1-4058-5266-1
Multi-Rom ISBN: 978-1-4058-5265-4
Pack ISBN: 978-1-4058-6697-2

Printed in China GCC/01
Illustrations and cover by Mackerel Design
Designed and Project Managed by Starfish Design